GREAT AMERICAN

HORSES

AN IMAGINATION LIBRARY SERIES

TENNESSEE WALKING
HORSES

by Victor Gentle and Janet Perry

Gareth Stevens Publishing
A WORLD ALMANAC EDUCATION GROUP COMPANY

For Tave, another Southern gentleman. And for Yucui, whose subtle yet significant talents are appreciated.

—Victor Gentle and Janet Perry

Please visit our web site at: www.garethstevens.com
For a free color catalog describing Gareth Stevens' list of high-quality books and multimedia programs, call 1-800-542-2595 (USA) or 1-800-461-9120 (Canada). Gareth Stevens Publishing's Fax: (414) 332-3567.

Library of Congress Cataloging-in-Publication Data

Gentle, Victor.
    Tennessee walking horses / by Victor Gentle and Janet Perry.
        p. cm. — (Great American horses: an imagination library series)
    Includes bibliographical references (p. 23) and index.
    ISBN 0-8368-2940-9 (lib. bdg.)
    1. Tennessee walking horse—Juvenile literature. [1. Tennessee walking horse.
2. Horses.] I. Perry, Janet, 1960- II. Title.
SF293.T4G46   2001
636.1'3—dc21   2001020849

First published in 2001 by
Gareth Stevens Publishing
A World Almanac Education Group Company
330 West Olive Street, Suite 100
Milwaukee, WI 53212 USA

Text: Victor Gentle and Janet Perry
Page layout: Victor Gentle, Janet Perry, and Scott M. Krall
Cover design: Renee M. Bach
Series editor: Katherine J. Meitner
Picture researcher: Diane Laska-Swanke

Photo credits: Cover, pp. 5, 7, 9, 21, 22 © Bob Langrish; p. 11 Courtesy of Kim Abney, Abney Art, and the Tennessee Walking Horse Breeders and Exhibitors Association; p. 13 © Arthur Hill/Visuals Unlimited; p. 15 Photofest; p. 17 Courtesy of Jack Greene; p. 19 Courtesy of Sgt. J. D. Harber of the Metro Nashville Police Department Mounted Patrol

Printed in the United States of America

1 2 3 4 5 6 7 8 9 05 04 03 02 01

Front cover: A spirited Tennessee Walking Horse shows how to make it easy for the rider, who only needs to sit straight and smile.

TABLE OF CONTENTS

Words that appear in the glossary are printed in **boldface** type the first time they occur in the text.

NICE AND EASY

Riding a Tennessee Walking Horse is like riding a swiftly floating cloud. Its **running walk** is smooth enough to ride for days. Its sweet personality soothes the most timid riders. These gentle, stately horses have been **bred** for these fine qualities.

Americans starting farms in Tennessee during the 1800s carefully chose **mares** and **stallions** that were easy to handle and a delight to ride. Then they bred them and created the Tennessee Walking Horse. These special horses stepped lightly around plants, were smooth to ride, and could pull wagons.

With horses like these, Tennessee farmers could easily manage large farms.

Also known as "turn-row" horses or plantation walking horses, the early Walkers were smooth. Today they are great ranch horses, like this one.

EASY RIDING

The running walk is the Tennessee Walking Horse's main feature.

Plain walking, for all horses, has four steps — that is, left back, right front, right back, left front. During this type of walk, the rider is bounced slightly as the horse drops its weight onto each hoof.

The running walk is different. It has the same number of steps, but each hind hoof is placed in front of the footprint made by each front hoof. The weight of the horse is moved smoothly from back foot to front. It is also faster. A walk is about 4 miles (6.4 kilometers) per hour. A running walk can be 10 to 20 miles (16 to 32 km) per hour.

The "rocking chair canter" is another easy-to-ride **gait** that Walking Horses can do. This one gives it a whirl.

EASY GOING

How did Tennessee Walking Horses get so great? From the late 1700s to the 1800s, Americans bred several great horse **breeds** together to give the Tennessee Walking Horse its fine features.

Standardbreds gave them strength, endurance, and size. Morgans and Saddlebreds gave them style and grace. All three breeds combined gave them their easy-going nature. These breeds were also gaited. That means they could do more than walk, trot, and **gallop**.

In 1886, the **foundation sire** for the Tennessee Walking Horse breed was born. He was a failure as a racehorse. His name was Black Allan.

A Walker's winning features are strong shoulders, a sturdy back, straight legs, and a sweet face. They are all here.

HIDDEN TREASURE

Black Allan's father was a Standardbred. His mother was a Morgan. He was bred to be a winning racehorse.

Black Allan began his races by **pacing** far ahead of the pack. When he tried to speed up, he lost control of his legs. He could not win no matter how hard he tried. As a result, he was sold many times. He was even traded for mules. Each of his many owners loved his gentleness, but they wanted a winner, so he was sold again and again.

Finally Black Allan arrived in Tennessee, where a new owner understood him. There, his colts won horse shows right and left. Suddenly, everyone wanted foals with Black Allan's classy, gliding **gaits**.

Black Allan was a gleaming black stallion with a streak of white on his face. His good looks and gentle manner were famous.

HARD TO MISS

Black Allan began his life by disappointing his owners. Before he died, he was the father of a whole breed of magnificent Tennessee Walkers.

Tennessee Walking Horses have many traits that make them easy to see *and hear*. Besides their special running walk, they sometimes nod their heads and click their teeth — like a one-horse band.

Their conformation is balanced, which means their legs, chest, and back fit neatly with each other. Their height is also about the same as their length.

Tennessee Walking Horses are comfortable to ride and are eye-catching, too.

The horse's mouth is a little open in this picture. Do you think it is pulling on the bit or clicking its teeth?

NICE WORK

Trigger and Champion were famous TV and movie horses. Their shows were so successful that they outlasted the horses that starred in them. The original Trigger and Champion retired. What horses would you replace these old stars with? Tennessee Walking Horses, of course!

Trigger Jr. and Champion Jr. were both Tennessee Walkers. Their cowboy costars loved their smooth styles and could trust these horses to be patient through long days of shooting movies. Besides, these horses were really cute!

Champion Jr. seemed destined for fame. He was even born on the same day that Charles Lindbergh made his historic flight from New York to Paris.

Champion Jr.'s real name was Lindy. He was named after the famous airplane pilot, Charles Lindbergh.

HARD TO BEAT

John and Daniel Starnes are lucky brothers. They own two winning Walkers. Travlin Victory Ann, or "Annie," and her daughter, Traveling Time, do much more than walk. John and Annie won the Superior Youth Versatility Championship in 1996. Dan and Traveling Time won in 1999. To win, the boys had to compete in twelve different events.

One of these events was the water glass class. In this class, the horse uses different gaits while the rider holds a full glass of water. Whoever spills the least, wins.

"That's the toughest one," Dan says.

John barrel races to earn points for the Championship. He must gallop Annie around three barrels faster than anyone else!

WALKING NEW PATHS

Tennessee Walking Horses have always been valuable work horses. Ever since Walkers were developed as a breed, farmers, cowboys, ranchers, and trail riders have all found them fun to ride — no matter how long their rides were.

Times have changed. Most Americans use cars to get around. Walkers, however, make great working horses for police patrols and **physical therapists**. They are easy to ride on long patrols and stay calm in noisy crowds and traffic.

The easy ride and gentle personality of a Tennessee Walking Horse might be the best way for people with disabilities to get outdoor exercise — with some help from a strong friend.

The Metro Police Explorers get a ride on the Nashville Metro Police Tennessee Walking Horses.

THE WALKING LIFE

Black Allan's offspring have done a great job proving that he was not a failure, but a success. His sons left their mark on winning show horses for a hundred years. The style everyone admired in him has been captured on television and in the movies.

Like Black Allan, Walkers can do many different things. They step lightly through slippery rocks on wilderness trails, smoothly carry police around rough city streets, and sweetly accept hugs from timid riders.

All of Black Allan's gentleness and class lives on in every Tennessee Walking Horse — whatever its walk of life.

Tennessee Walking foals look great when they trot, too! What career waits for this youngster? Police or show horse? Or plain old pasture pal?

DIAGRAM AND SCALE OF A HORSE

Here's how to measure a horse with a show of hands. Tennessee Walking Horses, like this one, come in many colors.

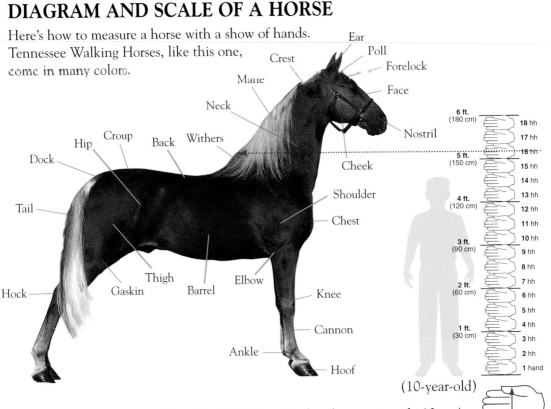

1 hand high (hh) = 4 inches (approximately 10 cm)

(10-year-old)

WHERE TO WRITE OR CALL FOR MORE INFORMATION

Tennessee Walking Horse Breeders' & Exhibitors' Association
P. O. Box 286
Lewisburg, TN 37091-0286
Phone: (931) 359-1574, (800) 359-1574

MORE TO READ AND VIEW

Books (Fiction): *Changing Times: The Story of a Tennessee Walking Horse.* Deborah Felder (Gareth Stevens)

Books (Nonfiction): *The Complete Guides to Horses and Ponies* (series). Jackie Budd (Gareth Stevens)
DK Riding Club: Horse and Pony Breeds. Carolyn Henderson (Dorling Kindersley)
Great American Horses (series). Victor Gentle and Janet Perry (Gareth Stevens)
They Dreamed of Horses: Careers for Horse Lovers. Kay Frydenborg (Walker & Co.)

Magazines: *Horse Illustrated* and its new magazine for young readers, *Young Rider*
Voice of the Tennessee Walking Horse

Videos (Nonfiction): *Eyewitness: Horse.* (BBC Lionheart / DK Vision)
Noble Horse. (National Geographic)
Ultimate Guide to Horses. (Discovery Channel)

WEB SITES

Tennessee Walking Horse Breeders' and Exhibitors' Association
www.twhbea.com
  (click on programs, then youth)

For more about Tennessee Walking Horses:
www.walking-horse.com

For general horse information:
www.henry.k12.ga.us/pges/kid-pages/
horse-mania/index.htm

Some web sites stay current longer than others. To find additional web sites, use a reliable search engine, such as Yahooligans or KidsClick! (http://sunsite.berkeley.edu/KidsClick!/), with one or more of the following key words to help you locate information about horses: *Black Allan, conformation, running walk,* and *Tennessee Walking Horse.*

GLOSSARY

You can find these words on the pages listed. Reading a word in a sentence helps you understand it even better.

bred (past tense of breed) (v) — to have chosen a stallion and a mare with certain features to make foals with similar features 4, 8, 10

breed (n) — horses that share features as a result of careful selection of stallions and mares to produce foals 8, 12, 18

foundation sire — a male horse used to breed with mares to produce foals of a particular breed 8

gait — a way of moving. Walking, running, pacing, trotting, and cantering are examples of horses' gaits 6, 10, 16

gallop — a fast gait with a complicated four-beat pattern 8, 16

mare — an adult female horse 4

pace — to run in a two-beat pattern, where the legs move together, first on one side and then the other 10

physical therapists — people trained to help other people deal with physical injuries or conditions 18

running walk — a smooth fast walk, about two and a half to five times faster than an ordinary walk 4, 6, 12

stallion — an adult male horse 4, 10

INDEX